Rookie reader

Messy Bessey
and the
Birthday Overnight

by Patricia and Fredrick
McKissack

illustrated by
Dana Regan

Children's Press
A Division of Grolier Publishing
New York • London • Hong Kong • Sydney
Danbury, Connecticut

To Margaret Emily Haskins
—P. and F. M.

To Joe and Tommy
—D. R.

Reading Consultant
Linda Cornwell
Learning Resource Consultant
Indiana Department of Education

Visit Children's Press® on the Internet at:
http://publishing.grolier.com

Library of Congress Cataloging-in-Publication Data
McKissack, Pat.
 Messy Bessey and the birthday overnight / by Patricia and Fredrick McKissack;
illustrated by Dana Regan.
  p. cm. — (A rookie reader)
 Summary: Messy Bessey shows herself to be a true friend and a good guest
when she helps to clean up after a messy birthday sleepover.
 ISBN 0-516-20828-4 (lib. bdg.) 0-516-26411-7 (pbk.)
 [1. Helpfulness—Fiction. 2. Birthdays—Fiction. 3. Sleepovers—Fiction.
4. Cleanliness—Fiction. 5. Best friends—Fiction. 6. Stories in rhyme.]
I. McKissack, Fredrick. II. Regan, Dana, ill. III. Title. IV. Series.
PZ8.3.M224Md 1998
[E]813'.54—dc21   98-9223
                                  CIP
                                  AC

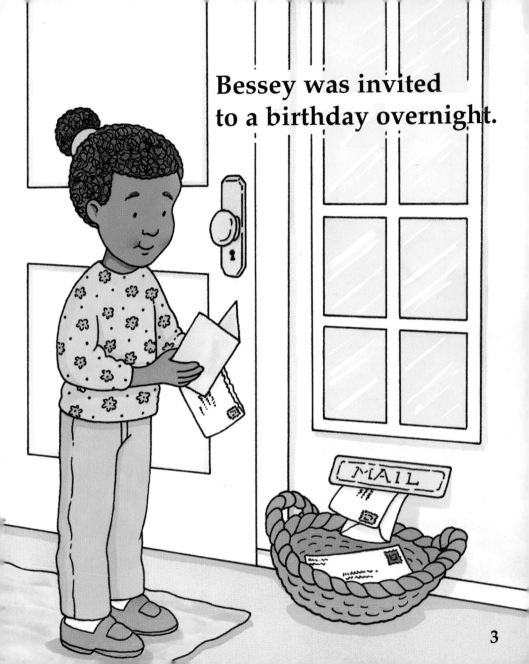

Bessey was invited
to a birthday overnight.

She couldn't wait to get there
to share that special night.

5

Bessey joined the others who came to celebrate.

6

They had fun eating,

drinking,

dancing,

singing,

11

12

sharing secrets until late.

13

Then Bessey told a scary tale
to everyone's delight.

But when she ended
with a **SCREAM,**
it gave them all a fright.

When morning came,
the guests went home.
None of them seemed
to care . . .

. . . that pillows, puzzles, books, and games were scattered everywhere.

21

**But Messy Bess remembered
what every guest should know:**
*If you helped to make the mess,
clean up before you go.*

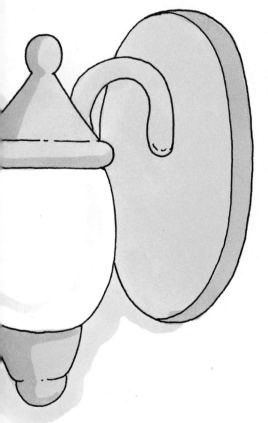

23

So Messy Bess got busy.
She found the mop and broom.

Nothing could be better
than to be best friends
with you.

About the Authors

Patricia and Fredrick McKissack are freelance writers, editors, and owners of All-Writing Services, a family business located in Chesterfield, Missouri. They are award-winning authors who have been honored with the Coretta Scott King Award, the Jane Addams Peace Award, the Newbery Honor, and the 1998 Regina Medal from the Catholic Library Association. Pat's book *Mirandy and Brother Wind,* illustrated by Jerry Pinkney, was a 1989 Caldecott Honor Book.

The McKissacks have written four other Rookie Readers about Messy Bessey. They have three grown children and live in St. Louis County, Missouri.

About the Illustrator

Dana Regan was born and raised in northern Wisconsin. She migrated south to Washington University in St. Louis, and eventually to Kansas City, Missouri, where she now lives with her husband, Dan, and her sons, Joe and Tommy.